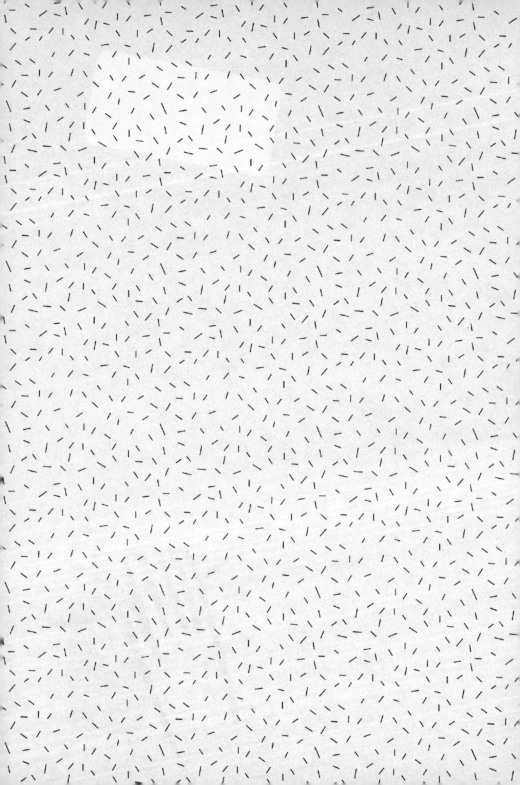

To every single young person
who has, at some point,
not felt GOOD ENOUGH
– this book is for you.
E.D.

First published in Great Britain 2023 by Red Shed, part of Farshore
An imprint of HarperCollins*Publishers*
1 London Bridge Street
London SE1 9GF
www.farshore.co.uk

HarperCollins*Publishers*
Macken House, 39/40 Mayor Street Upper, Dublin 1
D01 C9W8

Text copyright © Elizabeth Day 2023
Elizabeth Day has asserted her moral rights.

Text adapted from *Failosophy* with extra content.

Extract from Matt Haig's *The Midnight Library* (Canongate) on p12
used with the kind permission of the publisher and author.
Extract from Holly Willoughby's *Reflections* (Century) on p56 and p66
used with the kind permission of the publisher and author.

Illustrations copyright © HarperCollins*Publishers* 2023
Illustrations by Kim Hankinson.
ISBN 978 0 0085 8261 6
Printed and bound in the UK using 100% Renewable Electricity at CPI Group (UK) Ltd.
001

Consultancy by Dr Miquela Walsh, DEdPsych, MsC (Dist), BSc (Hons), HCPC accredited.

A CIP catalogue record for this book is available from the British Library.

MIX
Paper | Supporting
responsible forestry
FSC™ C007454
FSC
www.fsc.org

failosophy
FOR TEENS

A Handbook For When
Things Go Wrong

ELIZABETH
DAY

RED
SHED

Contents

Introduction

What is failure? Great question! It was one that I avoided answering for a while, because it seemed like such a hard thing to explain. But eventually the definition I came up with was that **failure is what happens when something doesn't go according to your plan.**

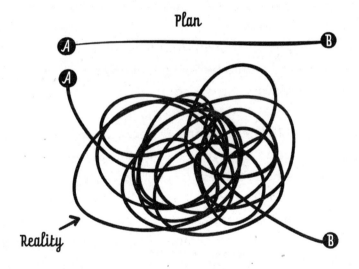

Plan

Reality

Failure happens to us all, even those celebrities who appear like shimmering modern idols on the red carpet and who seem to have everything sorted.

PERFECT YOU!
whitening toothpaste

Every day, we are bombarded with success stories to such an extent that we are in danger of believing that being exceptional is the norm. **We live in an age of perfection**, where we are led to think that we deserve success and will be rewarded with it if only we are clever enough or thin enough or sociable enough or, in some way, good enough. And online culture and social media have scared us into believing that any failure will be made public and everyone will soon know about it.

Your definition of failure depends on how you perceive success, but – here's the good bit – you can reframe what success means to you. Perhaps success could mean trying your best when playing football or hockey, rather than being the one to score all the goals? Or perhaps success could mean being nice to your brother or sister, rather than owning a pair of expensive new trainers? Or being happy that you are unique rather than changing yourself to fit in with a group? For me, the truest form of success is about how you feel inside yourself. If you're comfortable with who you are and how you treat other people, that's the best kind of success.

'You don't have
to BE the best,
just TRY your best'
— MABEL,

POP STAR

If we don't live our best lives for ourselves, we start to judge ourselves through other people's eyes, becoming people-pleasers. This means acting in a way that we hope will make others approve of us — whether they're total strangers, or our own family or friends — even when this goes against our own wants or desires.

As a teenager, I failed to see that my desire to people-please was making me unhappy. When I made friends, I used to think it was more important to be the kind of person they wanted me to be, rather than just being myself. I spent a lot of time trying to conform and doing things I wasn't comfortable with because I wanted to be liked. But of course, no one stands a chance of liking the real you unless you are brave enough to show who that really is.

People-pleasing sounds like it's a nice quality, but it can be quite destructive to our personal growth. **By constantly yearning for the approval of others and avoiding so-called 'failures', we miss out on the fulfilment that comes from being happy and confident in our own skin.**

'If you AIM to be something you are not, you will always fail. AIM TO BE YOU'

– MATT HAIG

AUTHOR

When I was four, my family and I moved to Northern Ireland. It was – and still is – a part of the United Kingdom, but not everyone there wanted to be part of the UK. When we went over in 1982, there was a civil conflict. We used to drive through a military checkpoint on our way to school every morning. Bombs went off frequently. It could be a scary place.

As someone with an English accent, I didn't fit in. In some environments, I was mistrusted because people assumed my family must be working for the British military, who were seen as enemy occupiers by those who wanted a united Ireland. (We were actually nothing to do with the army: my father was a surgeon).

At secondary school in Belfast, I was teased for my accent and I found it difficult to make friends. I felt very lonely and sad. My grades spiralled. I became quieter and quieter. Eventually, I told my parents how unhappy I was and I changed to a new school that suited me much better. Although that was a difficult thing to go through, I understand now that it has made me who I am.

I failed to fit in at my first secondary school. But there were benefits to that: I became an observer and a listener, which have proved invaluable skills in my later career as a writer and interviewer. It gave me empathy for anyone who is or has been bullied, and it made me understand the value of kindness. It taught me how important it is to make real friends who accepted me as I am.

It also made me realise that no matter who you are, there are some people who will always make assumptions about you that aren't true. But you have no control over that. Other people's opinions are mostly to do with how they feel about *themselves*, not about you. They might be unhappy or angry or have a difficult home life and they're lashing out. You are not in control of their opinions, but you are in control of your response *to them*. Don't waste your energy trying to change their minds. Instead, use that same energy to make a new friend or to spend more time doing the things you enjoy. Get to know yourself. And remember: when you go through tough times, it makes the good times feel even better because you have something to compare them to.

'THE DARKER THE NIGHT,'

Dostoyevsky wrote,

'THE BRIGHTER THE STARS.'

I have spent a large portion of the last couple of years thinking about my failures. The weird thing is that thinking as an adult about my failures hasn't been a negative experience. On the contrary, I feel stronger, happier and more empowered as a result.

When I use the word 'empowered' what I mean is that I can claim my own courage rather than relying on anyone else's. Imagine you are a phone. When you use a phone too much without charging it, the phone runs out of power and you can't text your friends any more which is really annoying. But now imagine that you are your own phone charger: an in-built battery pack that means you *never* run out of power. That's what I mean by feeling empowered. I have my own battery pack. I don't have to rely on anyone else to build me up. Failures can't hurt me as much because I know how to cope with them – even better, every time I learn from a failure, I build up my own battery life.

I'm no longer embarrassed by my failures because when I look back at them, I now feel proud of my resilience in surviving them.

For me, resilience is being able to recover or adapt when things go wrong, or when things change in ways I don't expect. Being at peace with failure in this way means I don't have too many regrets. I've accepted that we can't always understand why things happen at the time they're happening. But I do believe that life will generally teach us the lessons we need to learn if we are open to the possibility. This acceptance of failure helps me to be resilient and adapt when things don't go to plan.

I wish I'd embraced my failures when I was younger, rather than feeling bad about them. How different my teenage years could have been! My hope is to help you see failure as part of the bigger picture and understand that . . .

although your failures make you who you are, they do not define you.

And I wish I had been more open when things went wrong. I wish I had talked and discussed my failures. In my 30s, I was dumped by a boyfriend. I felt heartbroken and embarrassed. But when I confided in my friends about the experience, I actually felt closer to them. Being vulnerable is an amazing way to connect with others because the chances are, they will have gone through something similar but might never have had the opportunity to talk about it. I realised that conversations about failure were far more revealing than any other kind. When you talk about what's gone wrong in your life, you allow other people the space to be honest about their own mistakes too.

I then started to think about having these conversations more widely, so that more people could feel less alone. That was the idea behind my *How To Fail* podcast, which launched in July 2018. Each week, I ask my guest to come up with three 'failures' in advance of the recording. These can be sublime or ridiculous; profound or superficial. The only criteria are that the guest must feel comfortable talking about the subjects they've chosen, and that they are able to reflect on what they have learned from them.

My guests have ranged from footballers, psychotherapists, politicians, pop stars, chefs and former reality TV contestants. They have given insights into everything from failed exams and romantic break-ups to how to cope with severe anxiety. You'll hear some of their hugely inspiring stories in this book, along with lessons I've learned from my own life.

I have condensed the valuable experiences from my podcast and life learnings into seven key areas, intended as helpful guides through life's rough patches. Consider them the equivalent of having a chat with a good friend who wants to make you feel better.

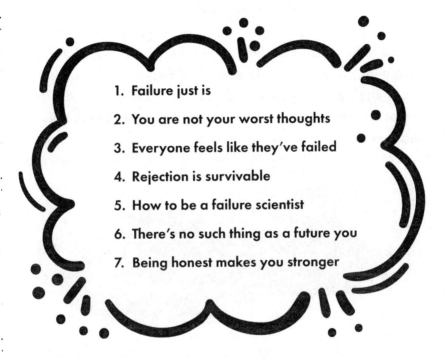

1. Failure just is

2. You are not your worst thoughts

3. Everyone feels like they've failed

4. Rejection is survivable

5. How to be a failure scientist

6. There's no such thing as a future you

7. Being honest makes you stronger

As Albert Einstein said, 'Failure is success in progress.' However difficult something might seem at the time, it is always possible to learn something. **Try to believe that something good will come from a failure.** Sometimes, you might not be able to make out what that positive is straight away. Sometimes, you can only know that with hindsight, but being optimistic could give you the energy or courage to do the things that make you anxious or worried.

I'm not saying it's easy. I know it takes a lot more effort than just talking to yourself in the mirror or collecting quotes from Instagram. **Our mental muscles require just as much working out as our physical ones.** Try out the challenges throughout the book to discover more about you and how to live your best life.

Some failures are far more traumatic than others and it might take more time before you feel better about what's happened. If you feel emotional pain – sadness, upset, embarrassment, anger – that pain is a fact, whatever the cause of it.

But there is a difference between pain and suffering. Pain, like failure, happens to us all. We accidentally burn our tongue on a cup of hot chocolate that is too hot. There is the immediate pain, which hopefully subsides quite quickly. Then there is the subsequent suffering, which lasts a bit longer as we struggle to taste food for a few days. But imagine being hard on yourself about the fact that you'd been stupid enough to burn your tongue for several weeks and months afterwards. That would be prolonging suffering unnecessarily.

Instead, you could say to yourself: 'Well, I burned my tongue, but at least I'll know for the next time to add a bit of cool milk to my hot chocolate before I drink it.'

Thinking positively when things go wrong will prove incredibly powerful on many levels. And instead of trying to avoid failure we can think instead about how mistakes actually help us learn and grow.

And that's what this book is all about.

So, read it all in one go, or dip in and out. Either way, I hope it might help you to realise that failure does not have to be alienating. In truth, it is the opposite: it connects us all. **Failure makes us human.**

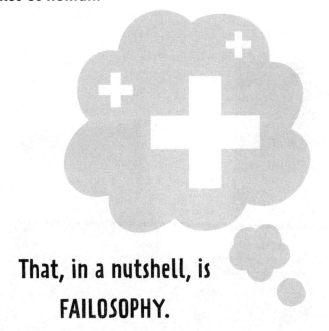

That, in a nutshell, is
FAILOSOPHY.

The Seven Principles
of Failure

Principle 1

Failure just is

This might sound obvious. Bear with me.

The first thing you should know about failure is that it is a fact. As I said before, failure is something going differently from what we had planned or intended. This will ALWAYS happen because of the beauty and unpredictability of life!

Failure, like oxygen, just exists. You can't wish oxygen away or live your life trying to avoid it because that would be stupid and impossible. Oxygen is essential to our survival and so, in its own way, is failure. Failure gives us the opportunity to learn, if we choose to let it, and that can help us grow into better, stronger people.

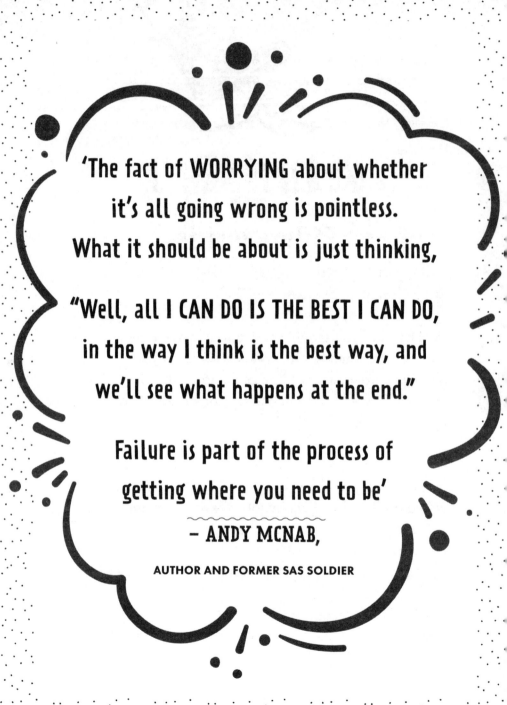

'The fact of WORRYING about whether it's all going wrong is pointless. What it should be about is just thinking,

"Well, all I CAN DO IS THE BEST I CAN DO, in the way I think is the best way, and we'll see what happens at the end."

Failure is part of the process of getting where you need to be'

– ANDY MCNAB,

AUTHOR AND FORMER SAS SOLDIER

Failure has happened to all of us and it will continue to happen to all of us at various points in our lives. There is nothing we can do that will protect us from failure for ever. There just isn't. Wishing it were otherwise is like wishing away oxygen. Or anything else that exists as a fact: shoes, for instance. There's no point living your life in fear of shoes, just as there is no point living your life in fear of failure.

> **'The minute you let go of that fear of failure, you score more'**
>
> **– ENIOLA ALUKO,**
>
> **FORMER ENGLAND WOMEN'S FOOTBALLER**

Failure is a fact. The emotion we attach to failure is separate but, to an extent, within our control.

RISE ABOVE!

Think about a recent experience that made you feel like a failure. You might have had a lot of emotions and feelings about it. That's totally normal! You probably already know that those kinds of emotions can make our body react too.

Write down a failure you've experienced.

Then write down your feelings around this failure, for example . . . .

sad

angry

EMBARRASSED

SULKY

hurt

Then try to answer these questions:

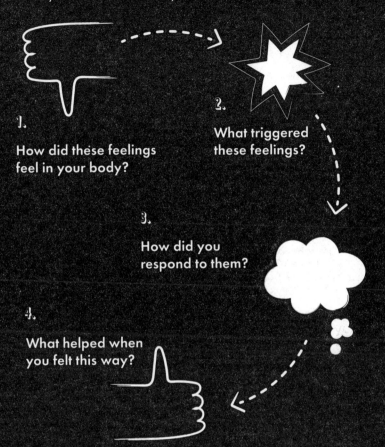

1.

How did these feelings
feel in your body?

2.

What triggered
these feelings?

3.

How did you
respond to them?

4.

What helped when
you felt this way?

For example, if one of the feelings from a failure was
anger, then it might make your body tense (1), it might be
triggered by feeling that you've disappointed someone
(2). Perhaps you responded by shouting (3) and maybe
what helped was punching a pillow, going for a walk,
doing something you enjoy, listening to music, or speaking
to a friend . . . (4).

Our failures may be different or they may be the same. We will also react differently to the same situations. For example, if the failure was losing a match, then some people might get cross and want to throw their bat/ stick/ball around. Some might want to hurry off the pitch in embarrassment and never play again. Others might think unkind thoughts about themselves, feeling more and more unhappy . . . Acknowledging and exploring these emotions, and accepting them for what they are, helps us understand that we can choose to react to them in different ways.

During one of my podcasts, former England footballer Eniola Aluko talked about when she failed to win the football league with her team. She felt devastated and was inconsolable on the pitch. As well as being upset, failing so publicly added to her humiliation. After the match, Eniola felt that she never wanted to play football again.

However, other people really helped her to deal with the failure. Her coach put practical steps in place to prepare the team for how to stay calm and not panic when losing a match. Her mentors, such as ex-footballer Linvoy Primus, taught her to see that failure doesn't matter if you've done your best. So she didn't quit football after that failure. In fact, a year later, she was named player of the match in the FA Cup final, which her team won.

Eniola told me that this experience had changed her attitude towards failure. She realised it could be a learning experience. She said: 'It's like, "OK, it wasn't meant to happen." Or there's a purpose for this or it wasn't for me or this door is shut for another one to open. It's completely different. I don't feel humiliated if I fail. I feel very much like, "OK, there's something in this . . . it's not going to be plain sailing all the time, especially if you want to be somebody great. You have to be prepared to fail sometimes and, you know, not get it right."'

It's important, also, to remember that failure is not what other people tell you it is. Your experience of failure is personal. As much as possible, it should be separate from the judgement of others.

People's perceptions are skewed by their own emotional, cultural, and familial baggage. When I was 10, I sat an exam called the 11 Plus. Whether I passed it or not would determine what kind of secondary school I could go to. I remember a neighbour of ours saying to me that it was 'the most important exam' I would ever take. Although I smiled politely, I didn't agree with her. I knew I would have plenty of exams in the future that were just as, if not more, important – including GCSEs and A-Levels. I later learned that our neighbour had failed the 11 Plus and had gone to a school she didn't like as a result. Her perception of that exam – and how crucial it was to pass it – was entirely shaped by her own experience. It wasn't shaped by mine. And it wasn't an objective fact.

Other people's perceptions are not always going to be the best marker of how you should live your life. This might sound difficult, especially in this age of likes and double-taps, but try as much as possible to **untangle your feelings about failure from other people's.**

We often want to fit in with others because we believe that if they like us, we will be popular and happy and safe. But there's a difference between fitting in and belonging. Fitting in is when you change who you really are so that you can be accepted. Belonging is when you are welcomed as you are.

When I was 14, a few girls in my year started smoking cigarettes (vapes hadn't been invented yet!). They were considered the 'cool' girls. I really wanted to be cool too, partly because of my unhappy experiences at my earlier school when I didn't have any friends. But I **also didn't want to smoke. I hated the smell and I knew it was bad for you because some of my family members were chain-smokers and had long-term health issues. So the real me didn't want to smoke cigarettes. But the insecure me – the one who yearned to be accepted by the cool group – wanted to pretend I did. I agonised over it for days. In the end, I decided to be honest. When I was next offered a cigarette, I just said 'No thanks. I don't smoke' and no one thought anything of it. In fact, they respected me more for being myself. So I became friends with them anyway.**

'It took me a long time to realise that I can't change other people. And I can't actually control other people. I don't control what they do. I can only control myself'

– TARA WESTOVER,

AUTHOR

I was taught to observe failure by Haemin Sunim, a South Korean monk, who is one of the most influential Zen Buddhist teachers in the world. His name means 'nimble wisdom', and the practice of Zen Buddhism involves looking inside ourselves for enlightenment. Zen Buddhists believe that we can only discover the truth from within, through meditation. We can't just buy something to distract us or think ourselves happier with clever words. We have to silence the outside world and become more aware of the inner one.

When I met Haemin, he was in simple monastic clothes –
a modest quilted grey overcoat worn belted around some
equally modest grey trousers – and he seemed so self-contained
that my chatter about the weather felt embarrassing.

**I was trying so hard to break the ice,
I hadn't realised there was no ice to be broken.
I didn't need to try. I could just be.**

Still, for the first few questions after I started recording with
Haemin, I panicked. He left such long pauses before answering
that I worried he had taken offence at something I'd said or
simply wasn't going to answer at all.

Then, when he did speak, his answers would be so short that I rapidly found myself burning through all my pre-prepared questions and running out of things to ask. He felt no need to fill a silence.

After a while though, I got used to his rhythm. It was calming. The chatter inside my head began to quieten itself.

What he was doing, I now realise, was allowing space for us both to contemplate what had just been said and what was about to be said. We were observing before we were reacting.

This, said Haemin, was the key to greater understanding. The whole point of meditation, he told me, was 'to become aware of what's happening in your mind. It is not to get somewhere, [to] some kind of peaceful inner state. Rather, it is whether you can become aware of what is really happening in your mind, clearly.'

So, I asked, is the next step to observe that without attaching emotion to it?

'Right,' he said. 'If you are attaching some emotion or expectation, then you become mindful [of that]: "Oh, I'm expecting something wonderful to happen. But it's not happening. I feel like a failure."'

The key to meditation, he continued, is 'to see yourself objectively in a non-judgemental way: *that's the* meditation.'

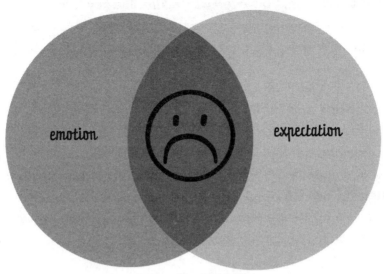

emotion

expectation

see self as failure

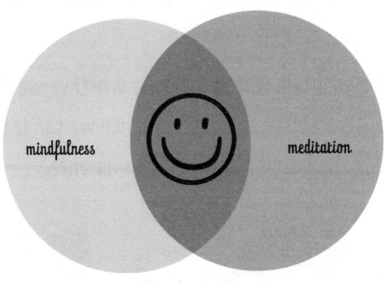

mindfulness

meditation

see self without judgement

It's the same thing, I believe, with failure. The key is to start by seeing it with an open mind, in a non-judgemental, unfearful way. To think about the idea of it before attaching any feelings to it.

Perceptions and feelings can often be unhelpful. They can come from panic, grief, disappointment and internal criticism. In a time of crisis, they are often not the best measure of what is actually happening. **These feelings will sometimes give us unhelpful advice** because they are automatic responses that come from past experiences, even though they might no longer be relevant to our current situation.

'Whenever we feel very unhappy it is because we are resisting what is,' Haemin continued. 'Whenever we resist what is, then of course we'll feel very unhappy. The trick is how do we turn our mind and then try to accept the thing as it is?'

He went on to say:

'We will fail. The question is whether we can fail gracefully and also whether we can learn something from that experience.'

PRACTISE AN OPEN MIND

Try to think about how you felt the last time something didn't work out the way you hoped. State the fact, observe your emotions or the situation objectively, then think about what you've learned from the experience and how it might be better next time. So, for example:

Fact: I failed in an exam.

Observation: I found it very tricky, worked very hard and tried my best but still did not pass. Was supported a lot by my teacher.

Lesson learned: Recognise this is a subject that is difficult for me. We cannot be good at everything. People were there for me even in this difficulty and gave me options for resits and doing other qualifications.

Next Time: I have more time to revise to do the resit, and I have a very clear idea of my interests and where my strengths are. I know who to go to for help.

Perhaps your failure has led to you being picked on. Perhaps you're not sporty at all and came last in a race. That can be so painful. It's OK to feel hurt and upset – in fact, it's important that you acknowledge your feelings rather than trying to ignore or bury them because that often makes it worse. Remember that these feelings – just like bad weather – do eventually pass and the sun shines again.

Once you've given yourself time to feel those emotions, then you can remind yourself that you are unique. We all have our talents and our good qualities: we just have to look in the right places for them. Even if you don't perform how you'd like to in one area, you still have other amazing skills. You could be rubbish at sports (I am) but you could also be really kind. You could find it difficult to make friends, but that might be because you haven't met the people yet who will appreciate you for all the things that you once thought you wanted to change. Stay strong in knowing who you are – that's the most precious quality of all.

Haemin taught me that you don't have to torture yourself about failures or be consumed by emotions. **Because you are in control of your perceptions, you have the chance to process your feelings in a positive and healthy way.**

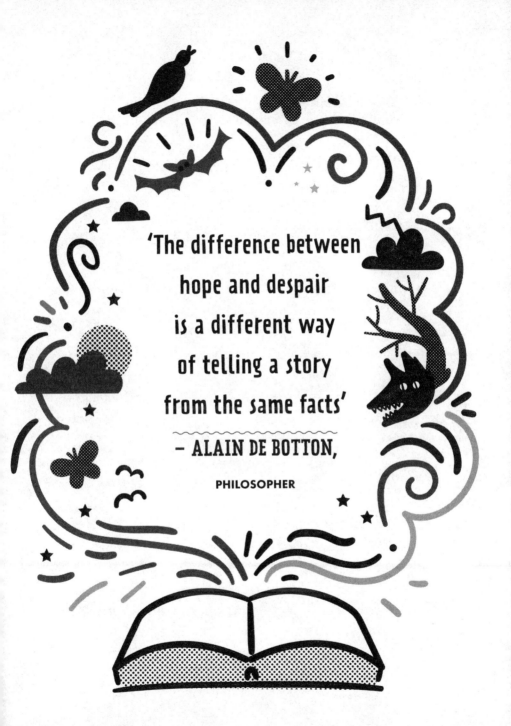

'The difference between hope and despair is a different way of telling a story from the same facts'

– ALAIN DE BOTTON,

PHILOSOPHER

Principle 2

You are not
your worst thoughts

In the past, I used to measure myself by external achievements, such as getting good exam results. Because of my lack of self-esteem, I believed I had to do this to prove myself worthy of love and approval.

I thought that if I did everything right,
no one would ever be able to dislike me
for having done SOMETHING WRONG.
And if no one else disliked me,
I couldn't logically
DISLIKE MYSELF.

Yet it never seemed to work. The thrill that a good exam result or praise at school gave me was temporary. It didn't protect me from heartache or loss or abandonment or being terrible at team sports. It didn't protect me from the failure I was trying so hard to avoid. It didn't make me feel that much stronger or more certain about who I was. Instead, **all it did was confuse who I was with the things I did.**

Gradually, I learned that **the voice in my head is not who I am.** Rather, as Haemin had taught me, it's possible for me to listen to that voice without letting it affect me.

Imagine switching off all your thoughts, one by one. The worry about whether you left your hair straighteners turned on. The concern about whether you're going to make the football team. The nagging feeling that your friend is cross with you about something you said yesterday. The decision about what you're going to watch on TV . . .

Would you still exist?

The answer is yes. If we turn off our thoughts, there is still an 'us'.

Once we take away the part of ourselves that has been created by the expectations of the outside world, we are left with an internal self that requires nothing extra in order to *be*.

And here's the best bit: **the act of simply *being* connects us to others.** How? Because when we stop disguising ourselves in order to be 'better' than we really are, we are more comfortable to be around. Instead of being the person in class who is constantly trying to impress everyone else, we can be the person who is at peace with who they are and doesn't have to show off. **Who wouldn't rather be *that* person?**

That's the theory, at least. Putting it into practice is harder.

'I took BEING PERFECT so, so seriously because I couldn't trust myself to still love myself if I made a mistake'

– CAMILLA THURLOW,

**CAMPAIGNER AND FORMER
REALITY TV CONTESTANT**

When I interviewed megastar pop singer Mabel for my podcast, we talked about her perfectionism and the fact that she never feels entirely satisfied with what she's achieved. She said, 'When I was younger, I kind of used to torture myself with it more, and it would become quite negative sometimes, whereas now I feel I'm channelling it into positive things by enjoying the moment as well. Where it's OK to have a day where you're like, "Oh my God, that was really sick!" and then move on to the next thing because you don't want to drive yourself crazy just never being satisfied with your accomplishments.'

'My biggest STRENGTH and greatest WEAKNESS is the pressure I put on myself'

– MABEL,

POP STAR

This is where Mo Gawdat comes in. Mo is the former chief business officer of Google X (the 'moonshot factory' where a group of inventors create new technologies with an aim of solving the world's trickiest problems by creating new technologies, such as balloon-powered internet). Based on his own experiences, he talks about his firmly held belief that everyone can be happy if they choose to be.

In his late thirties, on paper Mo had everything he could have desired: a flourishing career, money, a loving wife, two wonderful children and a taste for expensive cars.

Despite his material wealth and his family life, Mo was unhappy. No matter how many cars he bought, he was still depressed.

HAVE YOU EVER FELT THAT YOU WANT MORE?

Although you're not buying cars, maybe you want more of something? Another pair of trainers. New skins for gaming avatars . . .

Write down or draw what you really want. What thing are you desperate to have? What do you think will change if you get this thing? Is this more about not being truly happy with yourself and who you are?

Then ask yourself – 'is this realistic?'. Will this one thing change everything and make everything perfect for you? Realistically . . . no?!

Mo is an engineer, so he decided to approach his unhappiness as a scientific problem. The result was an equation for happiness, which states that **happiness is greater than or equal to your perception of the events in your life minus your expectation of how life should be.**

MY ACTUAL LIFE
minus
WHAT MY LIFE SHOULD BE
=
HAPPINESS LEVELS

Essentially, if you expect nothing, you can't be disappointed. Whereas if you expect too much or if you have FIXED expectations, you'll always feel dissatisfied.

To put this theory into practice, Mo said,

'You have to accept that your brain is an organ you have the ability to control.'

Your thoughts are a biological product of your brain in much the same way that the blood pumped around your body is a biological product of your heart. You are not your blood. You are also not your thoughts. So, you can stop your brain getting carried away with the panicked, anxious responses it uses to deal with confusion.

Don't get me wrong. Your brain is a sophisticated and useful thing, but not when it gets stuck in a loop of non-stop chatter because you're stressed. In these situations, your brain can sometimes misread the panicked signals your body is sending it as more threatening than it actually is.

When we're stressed, our brains tell our central nervous system that something's up. Our brains inform our adrenal glands to release the stress hormones adrenaline and cortisol. These hormones cause our hearts to beat faster and send blood rushing to all the important organs that will help us survive the moment of danger. For our ancient ancestors, this was really useful. If they were being attacked by a sabre-toothed tiger, they definitely needed their brains to help them run faster.

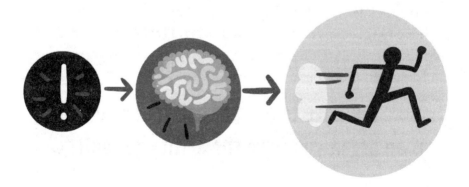

After the perceived threat has passed (the sabre-toothed tiger retreats), the brain should tell all systems to go back to normal. But in modern life, our brains are overloaded with so much information and stimuli that it can be difficult for us to work out what is a real threat and what isn't. Never mind sabre-toothed tigers: how many times has the smoke alarm gone off in your home and you've immediately thought it's a terrible fire, when actually it's just the toast burning? Or how many times have you overslept and been running late for school and you feel your heart might explode from your chest?

When your brain still thinks there's something to worry about, the stress responses keep firing. Your heart beats faster, your breathing speeds up, your chest tightens and your muscles tense. If this stress stays with us over a long period of time – days, weeks, months . . . then it can lead to serious health problems. Our immune system – our ability to fight off infection and disease – is weakened, making us more susceptible to colds and other viruses. Tight muscles can cause headaches and body pains and a raised heart rate contributes to high blood pressure, which can result in strokes or heart attacks. These health problems can arise because the longer stress stays with us, the harder it is for our bodies to return to a normal state of functioning. So the state of our 'normal' shifts to being on constant high alert state. This is why it's important to learn how to manage stress effectively.

Mo put it like this: 'Is your brain really that reliable if you let it loose? Or does it take us to places that make us unhappy and make us suffer for no reason whatsoever?' What he meant was that when we allow our brains to think that sabre-toothed tigers are around every corner, our brains will react in the way they know best. They'll alert us to danger and make us stressed. So we need to work out the FACTS over the fiction: what is a real threat and what is just our perception of a situation? We need to teach our brains the difference between a house fire and the toast burning.

Mo believes that if you are healthy in mind and body, **you can train your brain to think in a way that is more flexible and helpful to you**. You can ask it to take an unhelpful thought and replace it with a helpful one; it's simply a matter of practising.

'The primary cause of unhappiness is NEVER the situation but your thoughts about it'

– ECKHART TOLLE,

SPIRITUAL TEACHER

This is how Mo explains it: 'You tell your brain to raise your left hand. Have you ever had your brain come back to you and say, "Oh no, no, no. I'd prefer to raise my left foot"? No,' he continued, 'your brain does what you tell it to do.'

Mo calls his brain Becky. Here's what he told me: 'If you have a friend in school, Becky, who was so annoying that she showed up every seven minutes, told you awful things about yourself, made you feel horrible and then left with no positive impact whatsoever on your life, would you wake up the next morning, go to school, and say, "I miss Becky"? Would you listen to Becky when she speaks? What would you do with Becky when she starts to do that? You say, "No, Becky, please don't do this to me." If Becky starts to tell you weird lies you say, "Becky, do you have any evidence to back this up?" If Becky doesn't, Becky is a third party [and] you would say, "Becky, this is crap. You don't have the right to waste my life on crap." And that's exactly what our brains do. I stop in the middle of a conversation and I say to myself, "Becky, what did you just say?"'

In 2014, personal tragedy hit Mo's life with shattering force. His beloved son, Ali, died during a routine operation at the age of 21. At this point, Mo's conceptual ideas collided with the reality of unimaginable grief. Could he ever be truly happy again?

Five years had passed since Ali's death when I met Mo – and still, he said, 'Three to four times a week, I wake up in the morning or I go to bed at night and the only thought that comes to my head is, "Ali died." He is part of my heart. It's just I feel that part of me is missing.'

This is the message his brain still gives him.

'I answer in a very simple way,' Mo continued, 'and I say, "Yes, Brain. But Ali also lived."

'"Ali died" is a horribly painful thought. "Ali lived" is the same thought. But it's a beautiful thought. It's 21 years of joy, of wisdom, of learning, of insightful discoveries, of memories, of him taking care of his sister Aya, taking care of me, taking care of his mother, that I wouldn't replace for anything. Honestly, even if you tell me, "We will take away your pain for losing your son," I would say, "No, no, no, hold on. I want him. I want the 21 years."

'When I say, "Ali lived" I start to get memories that are all happy, all joyful, all the things that we did together. That's me being the boss. That's me telling my brain to take charge, so that if there is something we can do, we do it. If there isn't, then don't torture me, because there is no point torturing me if there is nothing I can do about it.'

Our worst thoughts frequently
do not tell us the truth.
Our brains create thousands
of thoughts each day
and most of these are not good.

They can be the product of grief or panic or sadness or
a defence mechanism — an automatic response we use to
protect ourselves (for instance, some people might crack a joke
to deflect from the fact that they're secretly sad). These defence
mechanisms are often formed by past memories that have
outlived their usefulness. Our thoughts can take on the voices
of harsh parents or disapproving teachers, or an internal critic
who warns us about getting too big for our boots.

But what evidence do they have for what they're saying?
**We are in charge of interrogating how true our thoughts
are and of changing the way we speak to ourselves.**

REALITY CHECK!

Step 1: Think of situations that you find difficult and write one of them down.

Step 2: What worried thoughts and unwelcome messages from your brain come from your answer to step 1? Write them down too.

Step 3: Now write down how these unwelcome messages have made you feel.

Here's an example of one of my challenging situations:

Step 1 Answer: Sitting my Chemistry exam when I was 11.

Step 2 Answer: I'm terrible at Science. I'm going to make loads of mistakes. People will laugh at me when the results come out. I'll let my parents down. Everyone will think I'm stupid.

Step 3 Answer: I feel panicked, anxious and upset. My stomach is in knots and I feel like I might throw up.

Look back at your answer for step 2. Compare it with what your parents/friends/teachers might say to you if you told them your thoughts. Can you see that there are different ways of thinking about the same situation?

Then go back to your answer to step 3. Have your feelings changed? Are those unwelcome messages feeling a bit less horrible now that you have thought about what your parents, friends or teachers might say instead?

When I invited author and TV presenter Holly Willoughby onto the podcast, she told me about her way of transforming a negative thought. Her focus was on envy or jealousy. In Holly's book she mentions 'repackaging jealousy as possibility' and she said: 'It came to me because I think we are obsessed with comparison, really, and sometimes a bit of healthy competition is good because it keeps us nudging along, if you like. It's good to have a dream . . . I don't want to use this to batter social media with because I exist quite a lot on social media and I love it. But there are parts of it that are tricky and difficult and I think seeing other people living out extraordinary, glamorous lives – or it could be a friend that maybe suddenly has met the man of her dreams and you're single – and you're finding that really difficult.

'I think jealousy is a really natural emotion and I think quite often these emotions, these difficult emotions . . . are things that we try to suppress, that we're somehow bad for feeling them and we shouldn't be feeling them. But I think, sometimes, if you look at something like jealousy what it actually does is show you that there is something that you would like to be in your life that currently isn't.

'But instead of seeing it as a bad thing . . . you could go, "Right, well, obviously in my life I would like that because it's making me feel bad that I haven't got it – in fact it's making me dislike the other person because I haven't got what they've got – but actually if I repackage this in my head, quite simply **they're showing me that there is all this possibility . . . there is something for everybody if you want to go out and get it or work towards it.**" I'm not going to say it necessarily happens, but the *possibility* is there. So I think, actually, it can be quite a hopeful feeling.'

Holly explained that 'negative' feelings can reveal something important about ourselves. Instead of being swallowed up by the harmful and damaging emotion or blaming other people for it, we could try and ask ourselves what that feeling is trying to tell us. Approached in this way, rethinking and reevaluating circumstances that would usually make you feel bad can actually be very uplifting.

Principle 3

Everyone feels like they've failed

In this age of social media, everyone *seems* to be doing far better than we are.

Humans have always compared themselves to other people. Historically, this helped us measure our abilities for survival within a social group. One theory is that our ancient ancestors found safety in numbers. Being members of a tribe who looked out for each other offered greater protection than trying to survive on our own. It also meant that we could see things in others that we wanted for ourselves. Perhaps one tribe member had an animal fur that kept them warm in winter, while you shivered through the colder months. That comparison – or envy – might prompt you to find an animal fur for yourself. If a whole group of people wore animal furs, you might start to feel left out and the desire to get one for yourself would become even stronger. The ultimate goal – to get a fur for yourself – would help you stay alive.

Still, it's very difficult to present this as fact given that no one really knows what went on in prehistoric minds! What we do know is that we all have 'unconscious bias' – an automatic way of preferring people who are similar to us. Because this is 'unconscious' we are often unaware of it and as it is automatic, it can be difficult to control.

Hundreds of years ago, people felt safer with others they thought were similar to them. Those who didn't fit in – for reasons of race, religion or geography – were viewed as a threat. War, colonialism, religious conflict and political disagreement can all be seen through this lens.

These days, we happily live in a different era, where we are rightly encouraged to look for connections between people because we've realised there is more that links us than sets us apart. Comparison is harmful because it can create division and conflict. Connection, by contrast, fosters healthy relationships with other people, countries and faiths.

But although we know comparison can be negative, we've allowed it to run rampant. In the modern world, we are not just comparing ourselves to our tribal members, but to a whole world of people documenting their lives online.

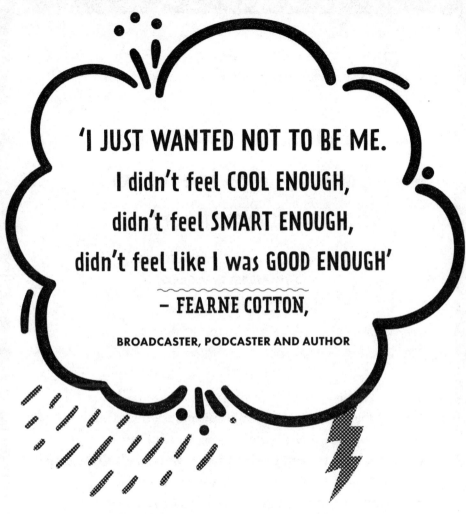

'I JUST WANTED NOT TO BE ME.
I didn't feel COOL ENOUGH,
didn't feel SMART ENOUGH,
didn't feel like I was GOOD ENOUGH'

– FEARNE COTTON,

BROADCASTER, PODCASTER AND AUTHOR

This can sometimes feel unbearable. As you create your identity and work out who you are, it's much harder to do so in public. When you're stressed about making life choices, having the added pressure of pretending you have it all sorted by posting the perfect photo with lots of friends, or being bombarded by images online that seem to show perfect lives, can make you feel frazzled.

'CONTRAST is the thing that makes you feel like rubbish'

– STEVEN BARTLETT,

MILLIONAIRE BY 27, PODCAST HOST AND YOUNGEST EVER DRAGON ON *DRAGON'S DEN*

One of the most reproduced inspirational quotes is 'Dance like nobody's watching', to which I respond: **how are you meant to dance like nobody's watching when it feels as if everyone is watching, liking, commenting and judging your music taste?** How can you even find time to dance? And what if you're a rubbish dancer? Should you be taking dance lessons at the weekend to improve? Would that make you more dateable, relatable, successful, a better friend?

It's exhausting. But the people we're comparing ourselves to, the ones who appear to have it all, are in truth, not so very different from the rest of us.

Many of my podcast guests have faced difficult challenges too. When broadcaster Fearne Cotton came on, she talked to me for the first time about developing bulimia. She told me that handling fame in her 20s had led to a feeling of vulnerability because she felt 'over-exposed'. Her disordered eating was a way of trying to deal with that.

'It was a way of feeling like I was calling the shots and I was in control,' she said. 'And it's sad to look back and see that it was obviously the absolute opposite of that. I felt so out of control that it came to abusing my own body and it took quite a while physically to kind of move on from that. But mentally [it took] a very long time.

'It felt like a release. Like every worry, every problem, thought, was just gone. It was a little bit of euphoria afterwards. Of course it wasn't, I want to be very clear about that. But at the time, the mental state I was in, it did feel like that.'

When she met her husband and wanted to start a family of her own, Fearne decided she had to be kinder to her body.

'The reaction that I've had to that period of my life has been my thirties, which have been all about health and looking after myself and eating extremely well and healing and recovering and being on it with my health because I denied myself the pleasure of cooking and food for so long that it's now become my everything. So it's really important that that side of my story is really communicated because it's something I'm so passionate about and I know, because I read a lot of articles about it, there are so many people out there – men and women – going through this situation with disordered eating, bulimia, and feeling like they'll never, ever get out of it, and I don't define myself by being a bulimic. I'm not. I, for the last eight years, have been very studious with food and very careful about how I eat and how I cook and how I talk about food and I feel really good and recovered.'

Of course, if you'd seen glamorous pictures of Fearne at the height of her fame in her 20s, going to parties and presenting TV shows, you would never have known what was actually going on beneath the surface.

It's useful to remind yourself of this when you next compare yourself unfavourably to someone whose life seems perfect on the outside. The chances are that's not the case and they struggle with sadness, insecurity and failure like the rest of us. Every single one of my podcast guests has felt that way at some point in their lives too.

But here's the thing . . .

All those people who felt like failures survived to tell the tale.

For many of them, failing has proved a wonderful freedom, because they got to know themselves better and gained wisdom.

'I think that one of my SUPERPOWERS
is knowing that I'm flawed
and not being scared by that.

I've learned that those
cracks and breaks
you inevitably pick up during
the DIFFICULT TIMES heal stronger.

The more breaks and cracks there are,
the more OPPORTUNITY there is to
fill them with life lessons'

– HOLLY WILLOUGHBY,

AUTHOR AND TV PRESENTER

My personal progress when I was younger often seemed out of sync with my friends. I was always terrible at sport. No one ever picked me for their team in games classes and I was often the last one left standing before someone was forced to take me on, which was humiliating to say the least.

But one of my closest mates at school was brilliant at athletics, hockey, tennis – you name it, she was good at it. I used to find it really frustrating that I couldn't play at her level. When we ran races at sports day I quite literally couldn't keep up! No matter how hard I tried, I just wasn't as good as she was. It wasn't that I wanted to beat her; it was that I wanted to do the same things as her and to share those experiences alongside her. Instead, there was this whole area of her life I was excluded from.

In time, I grew to understand that friendship isn't about doing exactly the same things as each other all the time. It's about loving each other for our different strengths and weaknesses. It would be boring if every single person was good at the same things. Sure, my friend was gifted at sport, but I really liked writing. While she spent her weekends on the hockey field, I decided to set up a school newspaper. In sixth form, I was the editor and commissioned articles. I asked her to be the sports correspondent and she said yes. We both found a way to pursue individual passions and stay friends.

GET TALKING ABOUT FAILURE

Ask two of your friends or trusted adults about something that they feel they have 'failed at' and how it turned out for them.

If you ever feel lost – that you feel you aren't doing what you should be doing or that other people are succeeding more, better and faster than you, know that you are not alone. But by living through these times, you are learning valuable lessons about yourself and building a deeper pool of self-awareness and experience to draw from.

This will build up the resilience you need to cope with uncertainty.

'You should be trying a million things – especially the things you're not good at, just to see if there's some WONDERFUL little thing you can extract from the experience'

– MALCOLM GLADWELL,

AUTHOR

Principle 4

Rejection is survivable

Break-ups are horrible. I know this because I've had six serious break-ups and each one of them has well and truly sucked. Although I now know what to expect when a relationship or a friendship ends, it never stops being gut-wrenching, heart-breaking and soul-sapping.

After a romantic break-up, I question everything. I question my own judgement for being with someone who failed to live up to my hopes. I question myself for not being enough for the other person to love. I question society for its questionable messages. I question every rom-com I've ever watched, and I scowl at every loved-up couple I see in the street. **I question whether I'll ever find anyone I want to be with ever again.**

When a friendship breaks up, I obsess over what I could have done differently and torment myself with the idea of my former friend finding someone they prefer to me. I worry that I wasn't cool enough or fun enough or pretty enough or interesting enough to have kept their attention. I worry that I am, in some way, wrong. Friendship break-ups can be even harder than romantic ones because often there's no explanation. We fill that uncertainty with all our worst fears. We imagine them laughing at us with new friends or being mean about us behind our backs or deleting us from all their social media. Often our own insecurity plays tricks on us, but knowing that doesn't make it any easier.

Although I might not know why certain relationships or friendships ended, here's what I *do* know: every single time I've survived. And every single time I've ended up looking back and being so grateful for the break-up.

'The loss can be REAL, but it can still be the RIGHT CHOICE'

– TARA WESTOVER,

AUTHOR

Philosopher Alain de Botton explained to me that one meaningful way of looking at important relationships in your life – be they romantic or a friendship – is that **people are brought to you for a reason**. They teach you something you need to know. Once this lesson has been taught, you or the other person might move on.

This means that **a relationship is not a failure simply because it ends. Sometimes it is a success precisely because it has ended, and you have been given the knowledge you need to grow** (even if that knowledge can often only be identified in hindsight).

'Success is a personal perception'

– JESSIE BURTON,

AUTHOR

The secret to a long-lasting relationship is to keep teaching and learning from each other, to allow each other the space to evolve, rather than to waste your time searching for the perfect soulmate who doesn't exist.

You can apply the same logic to friendships. When a friend passes in and out of your life, it may be because that friend was needed at a particular time. Your friend might have brought you comfort in a time of need, just as you might have done the same for them.

> 'The OTHER PERSON has every right to REJECT you. It doesn't mean you are not good enough. It's just that it wasn't a good fit'
>
> **– HAEMIN SUNIM,**
>
> **ZEN BUDDHIST MONK**

In my last year at school, I had a boyfriend called Tim. He was really sweet and I liked him a lot but after our A-Levels, we were going to different universities in different parts of the country. I wanted to carry on dating through the summer because, well, as mentioned previously, he was nice! But he broke up with me. He was very sweet about it but said it didn't make sense to stay attached when we were both at the threshold of an exciting new phase of our lives.

Although I was sad at the time, I now completely appreciate that he was right because the break-up actually freed me as well as him. It meant I could do what I wanted over the holidays, including a girls' trip to Portugal that was lots of fun. And when I started university, I was grateful for Tim because I knew what kind of person I wanted to date. I'd learned what values and characteristics I thought were important in a romantic partner and what was important for me to bring into any future situation. I was able to use the failure of my relationship with Tim to give me necessary data.

When we broke up, it wasn't that there was anything wrong with the other person or with our relationship. It was simply that we were growing in different directions and were no longer the right fit for each other. What if every relationship or friendship could be treated in the same way – not as disasters because they ended but as opportunities to learn and evolve?

YOUR TURN

Have you experienced any friendships or relationships ending? Think about one or two things that you learned from this experience – write them down so you can remember and celebrate the lessons you have learned from something that had been difficult for you.

'I look back and I go,
"WHAT AN IDIOT."
But it's great because
I've learned from it
and I'll never do it again'

— VICKY MCCLURE,

ACTOR

Break-ups give us a crash-course in who we really are because when a relationship fails, we have to look at the part we played in it.

I can only speak from personal experience, but when I met the man I now love, I had been bruised by a succession of terrible break-ups and dating rejections. My big ideas of romantic love had taken a necessary battering. I was more realistic, perhaps, but I also knew what I wanted from a relationship, and I knew how to say that out loud rather than expecting the other person to read my mind. In short . . .

I had learned the necessary lessons from LOVE.

What I can now admit is that I could only have got to this point because of, rather than in spite of, the failed relationships I had experienced before.

It's true:

every single
break-up
has been
worth it.

Principle 5

How to be a failure scientist

'Through failure, if you're honest
and you see where you've failed,
how you've failed, then every time
you get a bit stronger'

– GINA MILLER,

CAMPAIGNER

When I started the podcast, I discovered that there was a gender split in how my guests viewed failure. In my experience I found that the women said that they'd failed so many times they couldn't possibly choose just three failures. But almost all the men said they weren't sure they were right for the podcast as they weren't convinced they *had* failed. I was astonished: there were people out there who, when they made mistakes, did not question their purpose or let it harm their self-belief. *What sorcery was this?*

As we've already learned, a feeling that failure negatively defines us is unhelpful because it doesn't. Failure happens. We respond. How we respond will determine how we feel about it.

When I interviewed the men, I realised that they weren't being arrogant. It was simply that they saw the world differently. If you're a cis (a term that means your gender identity corresponds to the sex assigned to you at birth), white, middle-class man, you are born into a society that is made in your image. For thousands of years, white men have ruled the roost. They were the prime ministers and presidents, the decorated generals and famous artists. We got used to thinking these men were born to succeed and in many respects, our current-day societies are still built around those assumptions.

Maybe this history has influenced how people of all genders have viewed failure. For many traditionally raised men, it can be difficult to admit to failure because they worry (wrongly) that it makes them seem 'weak'. They think they have to be macho and not show their emotions because society has taught them that men must keep everything buttoned up in order to rule and dominate.

It also means that if men encounter failure, they are either unlikely to admit it or they've been brought up to believe that failure is a perfectly overcome-able obstacle on their path to inevitable success. Sometimes it can be both.

If a woman, or someone who identifies as non-binary, or a marginalised person or a person of colour, were to face the same failure, they might believe that this is about *who* they are. Because they were not born into a world that was automatically friendly towards them and thought the best of them.

I'm happy to say that attitudes of many men are changing. In my podcast, I now have lots of wonderful men willing to open up and be vulnerable: Benjamin Zephaniah talked about his sadness that he had never had a child, for instance, and Ashley Walters spoke openly about his struggles with mental health.

Women are also feeling more confident in themselves as individuals who are not dependent on men. They deserve equal opportunities, just like all people should be able to have. And we live in a world where conventional notions of what a man is and what a woman is are shifting all the time. I feel so lucky to live in an era when gender is no longer binary and people have far more freedom to love whoever they want and express themselves in ways that feel fully authentic.

But it did make me think. What if, the next time we failed, we imagined the response of someone who would let the failure bounce off them like hail off a car bonnet? Would it be possible for the most insecure, self-questioning and sensitive ones among us to become just five per cent more like this?

What if we all
started to view failure
NOT as something that SINKS US,
but as something that can
help us RISE: a piece of
information that will help
us take our next step?

TRAIN YOUR BRAIN!

Get better at reacting swiftly and positively when a problem or a difficult scenario presents itself. It takes lots of practice, but you can do it . . .

1. Think of a difficult scenario, e.g. you didn't do as well as you had hoped in an exam, or you forgot the words you had to say in a school play, or you tripped over in front of everyone.

2. How did it make you feel? Rate it out of ten. With ten feeling the best.

3. Are there other ways you could see this situation, e.g. you know which areas you need to study for your next exam, or your teacher was there to prompt you with the words, or your friend helped you up.

4. How do you feel now you've changed the way you view the situation to be a bit more positive? Rate it out of ten again.

A scientist working on a cure for a terrible disease will try out a number of different strategies before hitting on the solution. If an experiment fails, the scientist does not automatically think they are a failure; instead, they acknowledge that the experiment has taught them something extremely useful by not working. They can eliminate the concept that doesn't work and get closer to the one that will.

It's a mindset that you can apply to many areas of life. Take exams, for instance. What if, instead of going down a rabbit hole of self-loathing when you flunk a test, you take a moment to stop, breathe, think . . .

'I realise now I could have revised in a different way to make sure I wasn't stumped by that one algebra question.

Next time, I'll prepare BETTER.
I AM NOT DEFINED BY ONE BAD EXAM RESULT.
I AM DEFINED BY MY RESPONSE TO IT.
I'll ask my teacher for help
on the areas I find difficult.'

In other words, what if we're cancelling out the stuff that doesn't work, in order to get closer to the thing that does? **Sometimes failure is not something to be avoided. It is something to be actively pursued.**

When I interviewed Deborah Frances-White, the host and creator of the highly successful *The Guilty Feminist* podcast, she told me about her early experiences in acting and comedy. She said that doing improv onstage in front of a group of fellow comedians was an intimidating prospect and one of the greatest enemies to doing it well was **fear.** Giving something a try is brave and courageous and if we fail then 'so what' because we have self-love and self-acceptance. **Love who you are.**

> 'There's something very FREEING about being willing to try something that doesn't work'
>
> **– MALCOLM GLADWELL,**
>
> **AUTHOR**

One of the exercises Deborah remembered doing in her acting classes was called 'Seen Enough'. The idea is that you get up onstage and start improvising. The rest of the class sits and watches. If anyone is bored by what they're watching, they leave. The performer onstage has to keep going until the room is empty.

'And at first that sounds horrific,' she told me. 'Of course! It sounds like, "That's your worst nightmare." And for that reason it's absolutely brilliant . . . [because] all the time you're ruling out what doesn't work . . . And I remember doing it, going, "I've got something! This is going to keep the audience!" And it became like a process. It wasn't about my individual talent. It was about what processes will keep an audience transfixed.'

Just like a scientist, this exercise enabled Deborah to separate *who she was* from the process of discovering *what worked for her.*

Her failures were a way to get information.

DETERMINATION TO DO!

Try starting each day with a phrase that will fight the fear of failure. Say one thing you know to be true about yourself, maybe something like . . .

I am strong enough.

I eat well for a healthy body.

I am a brilliant friend.

I work hard.

I am brave enough to try.

Say it to the mirror with a big smile, even if you are feeling anxious and unhappy.

Remember that we can do activities, such as acting, because we love them. We don't need to rely on other people's approval.

Years later, when Deborah was teaching her own drama students, she applied the same ideas she had gained as a 'failure scientist' to auditioning. She would say to her classes: 'When you're auditioning, your first year of auditioning out in the real world, you're collecting data. Don't ever go on an audition to get the job – go on the audition to find out how you best do auditions. How do people respond to you if you go in really confidently? How do they respond if you go in a bit tentatively?

'And every time you keep this manual, this little diary, because what you're doing in the first year after drama school is getting good at auditioning and discovering what process best works for you.'

By teaching her students that their aim was to collect data about auditions, rather than getting the part, Deborah had removed their fear. **The knock-on effect was that many of her students ended up getting the parts anyway because they felt no pressure.**

If we are able, as much as possible, to remove fear when we encounter tricky times, we will see failure more clearly for what it is: not as something that defines us, but as a missing piece of knowledge that helps us come closer to completing the jigsaw puzzle of who we truly are.

'We change and
we grow all the time'

– PHILIPPA PERRY,

PSYCHOTHERAPIST AND AUTHOR

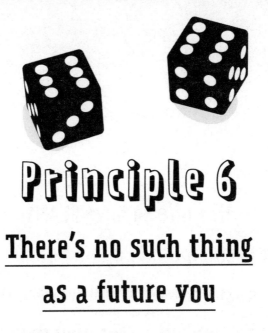

Principle 6

There's no such thing as a future you

I used to be someone with a detailed five-year plan. I would know where I would be living, what job I'd be pursuing, the precise brand of coffee I would drink every morning.

There was only one problem. **The plan never worked.**

Because by the time I got to that projected five-year point, I was never quite the person I had thought I would be. I would be living in a different country. I'd have given up drinking coffee altogether . . .

After a while, I realised that instead of reassuring me and giving me a clear focus, **my five-year plans were actually making me feel like a failure for not living up to my own expectations.**

'It's nice to have PLANS,
but even a plan C, D and E sometimes
doesn't cover the unexpected.
So being OPEN to the opportunities
that can come, and to roll with them,
is really important'

– MEERA SYAL,

**ACTOR, COMEDIAN,
PLAYWRIGHT AND AUTHOR**

I was setting my standards far too high, with a far too narrow outlook, and I was disappointed when I didn't achieve my aims within the time span I had chosen.

It's partly why I don't like New Year's resolutions. **We live in a culture that celebrates impossible perfection.** We are fed the lie that aspiration and ambition can only be found in our desire for unobtainable things – new cars, new clothes, new homes, new selves – when, in fact, **we can motivate ourselves in a different way, by seeking contentment in ourselves as we already are.**

Do either of these resolutions sound familiar?

* **I will go to bed early every night so I can study and get my grades up.**

* **I'm going to go for a run every day so I can do a marathon.**

A bit extreme, wouldn't you say?

Often at New Year (and at other times too), we set ourselves impossible tasks, believing we will soon be better versions of ourselves, but it never turns out like that. After a few weeks, the new running shoes lie untouched by the front door. Bedtime gets later and later. And so on.

We have made ourselves feel like failures simply because the original plan was faulty.

In the rush for a narrow perception of what success and perfection are, we can ignore our own limitations and try to do too much.

But what if we were to change the expectation to doing what we enjoy? How about we tell ourselves that we'll go for a run or a walk because we love being outside and it makes us happy, rather than set an expectation?

What if, instead of planning for a future version of yourself that doesn't exist, you pay attention to the present you; the one who does exist?

The American author Kristen Roupenian said to me, 'I had this timeline that I had imagined for myself that had set points. I think that's super common, to the point where it's a cliché, where you're like,

"I want these things by this year and if I don't . . . it's too terrible to think about – I'll just be a failure for the rest of my life."

'I thought I wanted a lot of things I didn't actually want and I had just been telling myself all these stories about what would make Future Me happy, to the point where I was ignoring what present Kristen actually wanted and in fact could have.'

It's important that your thoughts about the future are realistically grounded in the present and that your dreams are true to yourself, not what society says you should want.

'Things can work out in ways you can't IMAGINE at the time'

– MISHAL HUSAIN,

BROADCASTER

Unless you can add something practical towards your future growth right now, there's no point worrying about the things you can't yet control.

If you want to consider a five-year plan, a ten-year plan, or even a life plan, then make sure it's a really flexible one, true to you now.

The joy of being flexible is that it gives you space to follow your own passions when they come up, rather than being restricted by goals you think you have to achieve by a specific point.

I probably would never have launched the podcast, or written this book, or learned all this fascinating stuff about failure had I been sticking rigidly to my original five-year plan.

You'll deal with your five-year future self when you get to meet them. The possibility of the future lies in one simple fact: it hasn't happened to us yet.

WHAT DO YOU WANT TO DO?

Have a think about what makes you happy and write down some dreams that you have.

Then ask your family and friends what they think you are good at and what they think you'd like to do. Are there things that are the same? Are some different? Sometimes our friends and family can know us better than we know ourselves!

Principle 7

Being honest
makes you stronger

The most valuable thing I have learned about failure is this:
when we are honest about the things that really worry us – our
vulnerabilities – we create a connection with others and make
ourselves stronger.

Emotional strength is the ability to bounce back from life's
setbacks. And just like physical strength, it is a muscle that you
build up the more you use it. It isn't always easy. It's often not
the thing you want to do. But deciding to face failure head on,
to process it and then to learn from it in an honest and open
way, is the key to living a more authentic life.

I went through a big failure in my 30s – I got divorced. My ex-husband and I just weren't the right fit for each other, even though I tried hard to make it work. When our marriage ended, I was worried about letting my family down, and all the guests who had come to our wedding and given us generous gifts. I thought they'd be disappointed in me and I was scared about the unknowable future that lay ahead. But what I discovered is that the people who really loved me understood without my even having to explain. I realised that because my life had veered off the course I'd planned for myself, I needed to take time to understand who I now was and what kind of life I truly wanted next. I didn't want to fall into the same trap of trying to please other people and forgetting my own ambitions and needs. I booked an Airbnb and went to live in a different city for three months. Being somewhere else, where no one knew me, gave me the clarity I needed. I made the effort to spend some time with myself.

Getting to know yourself is really important because when you do that, you nurture internal confidence and self-worth. It means that when you make new friends or strike up new relationships, the other person is much clearer about what they're getting and you are no longer scared of saying what you want.

You don't have to get divorced to start practising this! You can start small. Perhaps instead of wearing something that other people do just so that you can fit in, you could wear something that you've chosen because you love it and it doesn't matter what other people think. Most people aren't looking at you half as much as you think they are. They've got their own lives and obsessions to be getting on with. The best people end up respecting you for your individuality and loving you precisely for all those bits of yourself you once tried so hard to hide.

BE HONEST

Think of a time when you have pretended to like something or done something that you did not really want to do but you were trying to please someone or doing it for the wrong reasons. How did this make you feel?

Pretending to be someone else can make you feel that you are not good enough, which is not true!

Instead, practise 'I statements':

* **I like this type of music.**

* **I am finding this work difficult.**

* **I like chips with mayonnaise and I don't care if you judge me.**

Each time you use an 'I statement' you are sharing a part of yourself and being honest with others.

This also opens other people up to feel brave enough to be honest with you and that is where connection forms. The more you do this, the more confident you become in yourself and your views, and the stronger you will feel.

This is a life where you don't have to pretend, in which you don't have to remember what lies you've told about yourself for fear of being caught out. This is a life in which you can be honest about who you are, and where you are respected and loved for your imperfections. Imperfections are what make us human. They are what enable us to relate to each other.

> 'The ability to admit failures is ALWAYS an expression of STRENGTH'
> – DAVID BADDIEL,
> COMEDIAN, PLAYWRIGHT AND AUTHOR

Once you recognise your worries and choose to share them, they are no longer fearful things to avoid.

When we make a mistake, we can often feel ashamed. We might think that other people are judging us – as if they were expecting something more or better. We might judge ourselves and be frustrated and ashamed with what has happened.

Author and professor Brené Brown has spent years researching the sources of shame and how our anxieties make us feel vulnerable and doomed to failure. She defines shame as the belief that we are all alone and not good enough.

In a 2013 interview with Oprah Winfrey, Brené said that the solution was to talk about shame and to connect with another human being about what it felt like.

Another of my podcast guests, bestselling author Matt Haig, talks about how he wishes he'd shared his struggle with mental health and been open and honest earlier: 'I lost a lot of friends during the years I was ill by not telling anyone I was ill because . . . I wouldn't pick up the phone and so people drift away . . . I had a lot of self-stigma. I had a lot of shame about the word "depression".

'I really struggled and actually overcoming the stigma was almost, in my case, to a degree overcoming the illness itself because so much of the stigma made my symptoms worse because it stopped me getting help when I needed it . . . Actually coming to terms with depression was a big part of getting over depression . . . I had to get to a point where I accepted [depression] as an experience I was going through rather than a definition of who I was.'

It is the same with failure. If we feel ashamed of something that has gone wrong or start to define ourselves negatively by a mistake we have made, the solution is openness. It's always a surprise to discover how many other people have felt the same way.

This is why some of my favourite podcast interviews have been with people who are willing to be open about the darkest times in their life. And one that sticks in my mind is my interview with Camilla Thurlow, the broadcaster, charity campaigner and former *Love Island* contestant.

When we started recording, she revealed that one of her failures was 'not living up to Camilla Thurlow' – the idea of her that people had from watching her on television, rather than the real person she actually was, who often struggled with anxiety and feelings of self-doubt.

Camilla told me: 'I always get anxious before events, I always find them difficult, whether they're public events or personal events – I just really worry. But if I'm in a bad phase, that worry becomes almost paralysing. And then I go into a kind of avoidance technique, but I get panicked. And then I tend to be a bit . . . not more argumentative, but I'm more likely to react . . .

'But then there's also this kind of constant feeling of unease, just in general. It starts to become unbearable to be inside my own head all the time and yeah, I get completely trapped in it, trapped in a really negative sort of spiral, and I find it . . . it's hard to talk about this: it's not that the other option becomes any less terrifying, but when life becomes unbearable like that, you do start to think in a different way. It starts to change the way you look at everything.'

I asked her what she meant when she talked about 'the other option being terrifying'.

'You start to entertain thoughts of what not being alive would be like. And even if it's just letting that cross your mind or whether it becomes a more serious thought pattern, that's when you realise . . . it's not that that becomes less scary or less worrying, it's just that you can't see how this feeling is going to go . . . It's when you can't see a way out. There's no light because you don't think there's light at the end of the tunnel.'

Camilla said that although she was lucky to be surrounded by lovely, supportive friends and family, she couldn't always communicate what she was feeling. It was important for her to talk to them and open up so that they knew she was struggling in some way, but ultimately she realised the most important relationship in her life was the one she had with herself.

For me, I have found talking to a therapist a very helpful way of getting through darker moments. But I also have a technique which I call 'The Best Friend Voice'. I try to talk to myself as I would talk to my best friend. Often, our internal critics can speak to us harshly. What if, instead, we healed our hurt by talking to ourselves with all the love, compassion and understanding we'd give to our best friend or even a beloved family member or pet?

It's important for us to connect with ourselves, as well as sharing our vulnerabilities with others so that we no longer feel isolated. Because sharing our anxieties is the ultimate show of strength. **Being brave enough to share your wounds makes others feel less alone. In doing so, failure no longer isolates but connects.** This is a beautiful thing.

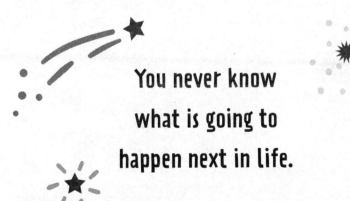

You never know
what is going to
happen next in life.

What Happens When Life Sends You a Curveball?

The problem with my definition of failure is that it doesn't fully tackle those cataclysmic life events that cannot be easily explained. A few years ago, Clemmie, one of my closest friends, had a brain haemorrhage and a massive stroke at the age of 38. Briefly, it looked as though she might not survive. If she did, her family was told, she would never be the same again. However, Clemmie not only survived but exceeded every single prediction made of her. She underwent major brain surgery, then had to relearn how to walk and talk. In the end, she was discharged from hospital less than three months after her stroke. Her courage and her love of life in these extreme circumstances were extraordinary to see.

There still is, says Clemmie, a long road of physical therapy ahead. I know she can do it because, well, it's *her* we're talking about: she has grace, dignity and courage in the face of a seemingly huge struggle. And she never questioned the unfairness of it.

But although Clemmie never asked, 'Why me?' I know that I did on her behalf. *Why her?*

The truth is, I don't know why bad things happen to good people. But I do know that . . .

the human spirit has an extraordinary ability to survive.

A journalist once told me that the Dutch have two words for failure. One is *fale*, which applies to common failures, such as failing an exam. The other is *pech*, which refers to a failure that is beyond our control.

Pech is linked to our word 'pitch', meaning dark or black, a term that comes from a sticky brown substance that was used in the sixteenth century to waterproof ships. The idea of *pech* can help us to understand that failure can also be a state of unexplained darkness, in which it is sometimes difficult to see any crack of light.

Whenever we experience failures that we can't control, we can do little to attack the failure itself. But we do have the power, however small, to shape our reaction to tough times. Yes, *pech* can be dark and difficult. But if we apply it in a different context, we can also waterproof our sailing ships so they are better prepared for the next thunderstorm. Resilience, forged through failure, can protect us.

That, in any case, is my hope.

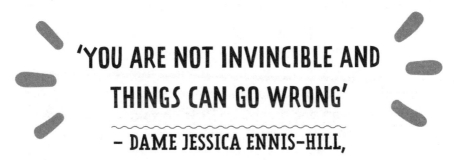

'YOU ARE NOT INVINCIBLE AND THINGS CAN GO WRONG'
– DAME JESSICA ENNIS–HILL,

ATHLETE

A FIRST-AID KIT

What's in your first-aid kit to help you get through tough times? Here are a few ideas to get you started:

1. A place where you can think quietly on your own, where you can focus your attention on yourself. Where is this space for you?

2. Something that makes you feel happy or energised. What is your joyful thing?

3. Something to remind you of the astonishing beauty in the world. What is the most awe-inspiring thing on the planet for you?

4. Thoughts that bring to mind feelings of love and connectedness. What do you think of?

5. Appreciating and being grateful for everything and everyone around us. How do you remind yourself of your responsibility to those who need you?

Here are a few of my first-aid essentials:

* **Going to a yoga class.**

* **Watching reality TV.**

* **Reading a book.**

* **Listening to music.**

* **Writing about my feelings.**

* **Stroking my cat.**

* **Soaking in the bath.**

* **Putting my phone on airplane mode.**

* **Focusing on helping other people.**

* **Talking to my best friend.**

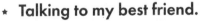

Athlete Jessica Ennis-Hill suffered from a foot injury in 2008 that caused her to miss the Beijing Olympic Games she had been training so hard for. We talked about how she felt after receiving the bad news about her injury. 'I was just so shocked and just so devastated that potentially this could be the end of my career when I hadn't even started, you know. I hadn't even got to anywhere near where I wanted to be.'

Sport is SO fragile. Even when you train hard and you are really gifted, things can go WRONG that are out of your control.

As Jessica said to me, 'That is sport. It's an awful, awful world. The highs are so high and you know you can reach some really incredible high points within your career but, like you say, in an instant everything can change and an injury can come out of nowhere and that's the end of your career and so it's incredibly fragile.'

When I asked Jessica how she got through this dark time, she told me, 'It was the people around me . . . my support team who basically said to me, "We are here to support you, to help you in every way we can," and to just help me just really gain perspective on the whole situation and it allowed me to just stop . . . It made me think about, firstly, what I'd achieved at that point and then it allowed me to think about how I wanted to move forwards and what I wanted to then go on to achieve and how much it really meant to me and without having those people around me to give you that unconditional love and that support that you just need in those moments, I think I probably would have just gone into myself a little bit and just said, "I might as well not do this."

Jessica also told me that she learnt from this experience about the importance of rest and that it is part of her training as an athlete. 'I was not for one moment going to let this take over everything that I'd worked for up to until that point. I had great people around me, I had all the support I needed, I had all the people saying the right things to me and no one really allowed me to take myself to that dark, dark place where I thought that was the end.'

After her injury and forced rest, Jessica came back mentally stronger and was able to take part in the 2012 Olympic Games in London where she won a gold medal in the heptathlon.

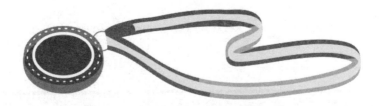

LETTING GO

Remember when last you faced a situation where something really upsetting happened that was out of your control.

Name the thought around this situation. Try and explain WHY the situation was so upsetting – what was the automatic thought that led to those difficult feelings?

Interrogate the reality of the thought: how realistic is it? Be honest and ask yourself if you are a) catastrophising (thinking something is much worse than it actually is in reality) or b) doing yourself down (being critical of yourself).

Think about what you were able to do in this situation. What helped? What would you do differently now?

Acknowledging that some things are out of our control is important for our mental health. How do you feel about this situation now? What has changed?

'It's OK to feel all the things
and not feel guilty about that.
So if I feel like I want to cry . . .
I just do that and embrace that feeling and
emotion, and not feel the guilt that I'm not
being a real man because I'm crying'

– ISAAC BORQUAYE 'GUVNA B',

MOBO AWARD-WINNING RAPPER,
AUTHOR AND BROADCASTER

Does Failosophy Actually Work?

Short answer? Yes, because I'm not preaching
a theoretical position. I have put these seven things I've
learned into practice myself so I know they worked for me.

I have tried for many years to become a mother. Very
sadly, I have been pregnant three times but on each
occasion, I had a miscarriage. A miscarriage is the loss
of a pregnancy during the first 23 weeks.

After my most recent miscarriage, I was faced with
a sadness that was out of my control. It was the ultimate
kind of failure – a failure of body, a failure to carry
a baby to term. It was a *pech* failure – and for me, trying
to cope with it was a direct challenge to put into practice
the formula I had come up with.

WOULD THE
SEVEN STEPS
WORK?

Spoiler alert: they did. They helped me realise this failure was something happening to me rather than swallowing me up whole. I could see that the failure existed separately from who I was as a person. After I'd processed the sadness I felt, this gave me a strange sense of calm. I knew there was hope, that if I gave it time, the pain would either pass or become livable with.

'Whether or not it is clear to you, no doubt the universe is unfolding as it should'

– MAX EHRMANN, *DESIDERATA*

One of the biggest things I learned was that we can fail, and still be at peace. That we can believe things will work out for the best while also coming to terms with the fact that our understanding of the world is imperfect and that, whatever happens, if we work enough on our strength, our resilience and our acceptance of failure, we will be all right. More than all right, in fact. We will be people who understand that life is neither wholly good nor wholly bad, but a miraculous collage of different experiences. Each one will teach us something worth knowing.

What Does Failure Teach You About Success?

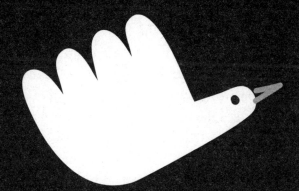

'Things that might otherwise
be perceived as failures, I very often
choose to perceive as something else:
as interesting, or useful'

– MALCOLM GLADWELL,

AUTHOR

I developed the seven things you should know about failure as part of a live *How To Fail* tour of ten dates in theatres around the UK (and one in Dublin). The format was loosely the same in each city: I came onstage at the beginning to outline each of the principles and I would then introduce a special guest and conduct an interview following the same format as the podcast, with three of their failures providing the central structure.

When I first agreed to the tour, I was extremely nervous. I was uncertain that anyone would want to buy tickets, and anxious about agreeing to big venues before we had secured the guests. I was worried that no one would have questions they wanted to ask, and basically that the whole thing would turn out to be a giant stress nightmare brought to life: the one where I walked onto the centre of a vast and lonely stage, only to forget everything I wanted to say and be jeered at by the few audience members who were there.

This fear never entirely went away, even when the venues started to sell out. The most extraordinary thing for me to get my head around was that, as time went on, we were selling out before we had announced the special guest (quite often this was because we had failed to get one, but shhh, don't tell anyone that).

'What's happening?' I asked my tour manager, Serena.

'Well,' she said, looking at me with her customary unflappable calm, 'I think it's safe to say they're buying tickets to see you.'

In February 2020, we sold out at the National Theatre in London and, however much I tried, I could not silence that internal nagging voice that kept asking me: *Who on earth do you think you are? Get over yourself, love. What have you done to deserve this?*

It was not the first occasion on which I had experienced **imposter syndrome – that feeling you are a fraud who is about to be found out** – but it was one of the worst.

I tried to analyse why this was. I realised I'd truly never anticipated the podcast or tour of *How To Fail* becoming a success and I certainly hadn't realised it would change my life. The more the podcast grew, the more I grew with it and the more able I was to be my true self in all aspects: professionally and personally.

To be rewarded for something that was already a reward in and of itself, felt greedy. And I think, at the root of this, was the lie that we are taught about success.

We are taught to believe that success will come to us with good jobs, wealth, fame, designer clothes and superyachts. We are taught to believe that success is external.

Success, we are told, is the ability to fly first class and gain followers on Instagram. **We've been told that success is to be known by others, when in truth the most meaningful success is to know ourselves.**

On the night of the National Theatre show, as I waited in the wings to go on, I began to wonder. Could it possibly be true, I thought, as I took to the stage and looked out at the packed rows of seats in front of me, that being myself was enough to be worthy of *this*? And could I have been so bamboozled by the lies society tells us about success that I felt my most imposterish at precisely the moment I was being most fully myself? Could my worry that I was about to be found out simply be an old, default reaction scrabbling to make itself heard? **Because it's hard to rewire your former ways of thinking, of being, if you've spent most of your life shaping the pathways of self-doubt.**

When we fail, our brains release the stress hormone cortisol. I mentioned cortisol earlier and, as we know, it fuels our fight-or-flight response to perceived danger. Scans reveal that when we're stressed, there is more activity in our reactive brain (the bit that wants to run away from failure) and less activity in our reflective brain (the bit that asks 'do I really need to run away right now?').

Imagine you forgot to stretch before exercising and got a cramp while taking part in a school swimming race. You come last. Your reactive brain would prompt you to burst into tears or be angry. Your reflective brain would say, 'Well, OK, I lost this race, but next time I'll know to stretch before I get in the pool.'

When we experience a win, our brains release endorphins, dopamine and serotonin – all the chemicals that make us feel good. This encourages us to do the task again. This kind of reaction is known as 'reward-based learning'. Simply put: if we are given a treat for achieving a task, we're more likely to want to do it again.

I have a ginger cat called Huxley. I think he's extremely clever and the most handsome cat in the world, but arguably I am a bit biased. When we first got Huxley, he was an indoor cat. There had been no garden in his previous home, so he had got used to staying inside. When he came to live with us, we got a cat flap installed in the kitchen door. But Huxley had to learn how to use it. So I put some of his favourite foodie treats on one side of the cat flap to lure him out. After a few tentative starts, he eased himself into the garden, gobbled up the treats and shot up the nearest tree looking very pleased with himself. That's an example of reward-based learning.

If you allow your reflective brain to take over, it means that every failure can be seen as an opportunity to grow. That's also a form of reward-based learning. There is almost always a positive you can take, even from the most miserable situation. Simply surviving and getting through a difficult time is a success in its own right. By choosing to see failures like this, we help our brains reinforce a more positive outlook on life.

The first few times you try to change the way you see the world and the first few times you attempt to look at failure as objective fact, rather than a negative verdict on who you are, your mind won't be used to it. It will kick back in protest, wrongly believing that the familiar ways are the best. But just because something feels familiar does not mean it is good for you. Often, it means the opposite.

Back in the theatre, the music dimmed. The stage lights went up. Yes, all this could be true.

Failure had helped me shed that skin of not-good-enough. Failure had stripped me back and built me up. It had broken me down and challenged me to grow. Failure, and learning how to deal with it, had made me more . . . well, *me*. The greatest realisation was that when I was most myself, people responded. They, in turn, felt more able to be honest with me. That creates an unbreakable connection. That is the solidarity of failure.

YOU ARE BECOMING YOU

You will be getting better at so many things every day. Some are hard work, but other things – like the maths you found so difficult at the beginning of the year – we don't even realise we're doing more expertly now.

Think of three things you weren't so good at at first, but which you're getting better at every day.

For example, mine are . . .

★ **Being brave enough to talk to people I'd like to get to know.**

★ **Remembering how to think positively before getting out onstage.**

★ **Practising being kind to my family even when they annoy me.**

American novelist Truman Capote wrote that **'failure is the condiment that gives success its flavour'** and it's certainly true that life is a combination of light and shade, and that you cannot fully experience its highs unless you have also understood what it is like to live through the lows. But I would go one step further and say that **in choosing to learn from failure, we also redefine our expectations of success.** Success for me now is about being able to be the fullest, most authentic expression of myself in all areas of my life and, in the process, forging stronger, more meaningful and more widespread connections with other human beings.

All of us can learn to fail better. It might seem strange or difficult or counterintuitive at first, but it gets easier with practice. With each failure that we choose to grow from, we become more ourselves. That, for me, is its own sort of success.

FAILURE continuously teaches us who we are.
It is nothing to be scared of.
Failure has been the making of me.
It might just be the MAKING OF YOU TOO.

A Celebration of Failures

Whenever a guest comes onto my podcast, I ask them to give me three failures in advance of the recording. I always find it fascinating what someone perceives to be a failure and often the choice is almost as revealing as the failures themselves. Some failures are profound, life-changing experiences. Others are less so. But what might seem like a trivial example on the surface – a failed driving test, for instance – can actually carry a lot of weight if it turns out the person in question got anxiety attacks every time they sat behind the wheel of a car (this actually happened with the musician and writer Tracey Thorn). It's my job as the interviewer to ask the right questions to unravel the deeper story.

I've put together a selection of my guests' failures here so that you can have a look at what kinds of things they choose to talk about. Perhaps, as you read them, you can think about what three failures you would choose and what you feel you've learned from them – because remember: learning how to fail is actually learning how to succeed better.

FEARNE COTTON,

BROADCASTER, PODCASTER AND AUTHOR

I failed most of my GCSEs.
At aged 15, I was probably working on TV, I'd say at this point two to three days a week, and then I would do school the other days. And I didn't really care when I was there much . . . I didn't really care because I was doing what I loved. And I couldn't believe that I'd sort of been plucked from obscurity to do this amazing job that was just so fun and so far removed from the first 15 years of my life where I hadn't seen anything like that.

So my GCSEs were not part of the plan but I did a few of them. I missed a couple because I was filming and I didn't re-sit them. I got good grades in three of them because I really enjoyed those subjects. And the rest I just kind of flunked. And although at the time I didn't see it as a failure, I think later down the line I saw it as this kind of social expectation and also kind of like a key to a door of this club I wasn't involved in.

The thing that I really passionately believe schools need to be more up on is soft skills. You know, soft skills in life can get you really far. If you work out what you want to do – and I'm talking about working as a team, either as a team leader or being in team, being polite, being kind, being a good communicator, making good eye contact, having good etiquette, all of these things that will seriously serve you well in life are completely abandoned for a very sort of old-school archaic method of learning. And there's still obviously room for all of those things, especially if you want to be a teacher, a scientist, a doctor, whatever. But if you don't, you are definitely made to feel like a failure.

Luckily my parents are very liberal and chilled and really hardworking. And I think that's always been the thing that they will fundamentally root back to: do me and my brother work hard at what we really love and what we love to do? And if we are, then great, it doesn't matter what it is.

And I'm really lucky that they gave me the space to just do it and try, and not all parents would have allowed that.

ISAAC BORQUAYE 'GUVNA B',

**MOBO AWARD-WINNING RAPPER,
AUTHOR AND BROADCASTER**

My AS Level results.
I open my results and I see 2Es and 2Us. I'm just in a state of shock. And I think that was the realisation for me, that I can't just cruise through life having a good time. I'd narrowly passed my GCSEs without really revising and I thought, *I'm just here for a good time*. And then the AS levels were a big shock to the system and made me realise nothing easy comes if you don't work hard. I ended up getting 1B and 2Cs in my A levels.

'Everyone's path is different . . . if you have an education, something you can fall back on it's great, but if it's not for you then find your tribe'

– EDWARD ENNINFUL,

EDITOR OF BRITISH *VOGUE*

STEVEN BARTLETT,

**MILLIONAIRE BY 27, PODCAST HOST AND
YOUNGEST EVER DRAGON ON *DRAGON'S DEN***

I failed at being in touch with my feminine side.
I see the masculine energy as being the highly competitive,
aggressive, cold, less caring or sensitive energy. And then
I see the feminine side of me as being more caring and
more emotionally in touch and those kinds of things. As
I've risen through my childhood trying to survive and fit in
on the playground, on the football pitch, and then through
business, I've really leant into that deeply competitive
masculine, emotionless, shut-up, doesn't matter how you're
feeling, let's just persevere, side of me. And I've come to
learn that that's really self-destructive over the long term.

I was this little rock. And that's probably why I survived
a lot of the harder situations because I was quite
emotionally vacant. But I've had to unlearn that and I'm
unlearning it as we speak. So I've gone on that journey
to open up more and to not allow the demons from my
past or the things that are in the back room or the things
from my childhood to be running the show as much.
That allows you to have a much more full life. You have
to have those meaningful connections. Toxic masculinity,
as I experienced it, as I portrayed it, is a barrier to having
meaningful connections.

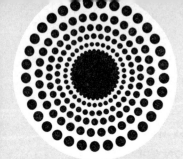

CUSH JUMBO,

ACTOR

Failure to be perfect.

I come from a big family, I'm one of six. Our family was unconventional to say the least. My dad was a very strict Nigerian who chose to stay at home and raise us while my mum went to work. My mum is from Scunthorpe and worked every hour she could to support us all. They met in their late teens and were both on the run from their pasts. They thought they could escape the past by building a future of their own. To them that meant having six children. To us that meant being brought up by two people who had a lot of love to give but not a clue how to parent or 'adult'. I was the second oldest and so, along with my big sister, 'deputy' of the family. I was told from a young age that my job was to be responsible, to lead, to set the perfect example for the others, at school, at home and in life. So I developed a fear of letting my family down, of not making them proud, of being a disappointment, and I've carried that fear my whole life, it's affected every decision I've made.

Recently, with the help of therapy and a wonderful husband and son, I've finally been able to start to kill this fear that has haunted me for years, but I still look over my shoulder for it constantly. It's a work in progress.

And in the last five years I've come to terms with the idea that being 'a deputy' in the family is definitely why I got into acting and performing arts. I am most definitely an actor because I get to be a child. I can pretend to be many people. At work people are usually laying out my clothes for me, telling me what make-up I have to wear. Making all these decisions that get taken out of my hands and all I have to concentrate on is playing, which I'm really good at. I know for a fact that I had to put some of that away, quite a lot of that away, when I was younger because there wasn't time and that a lot was expected. But at the same time I channelled all of those feelings into being a performer at such a young age, that I also think, 'Gosh, would I be who I was if I hadn't have done that?'. Because it was my escape. I can't remember a time where I haven't felt more comfortable onstage looking out into the dark than being offstage. I still feel more comfortable onstage than I do offstage.

Elizabeth Day is the author of five novels and *Sunday Times* bestselling memoir, *How To Fail*. Her acclaimed debut *Scissors, Paper, Stone* won a Betty Trask Award and *Home Fires* was an *Observer* book of the year. Her third, *Paradise City*, was named one of the best novels of 2015 in the *Evening Standard*, and *The Party* was an Amazon bestseller and a Richard & Judy Book Club pick. Her latest novel, *Magpie*, became an instant *Sunday Times* bestseller and was described as 'the most gripping psychological thriller of the year'.

Elizabeth is the creator of the chart-topping *How To Fail* podcast. She is also co-presenter of *Sky Arts Book Club* and has presented shows on BBC Radio 4 and Classic FM.

Find her on Instagram or TikTok @elizabday
or visit her website www.elizabethday.org

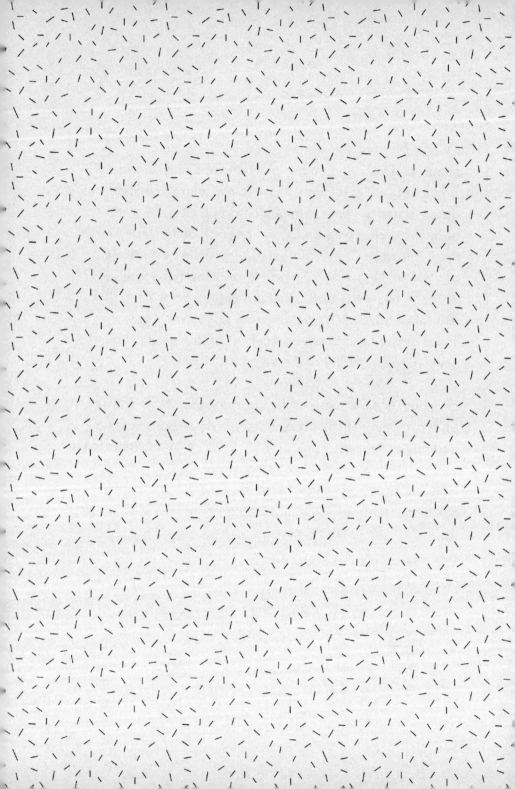